Buddhist Temple

Angela Gluck Wood

W
FRANKLIN WATTS
LONDON•SYDNEY

This is one of the symbols used
to represent the Buddhist faith.

For Marc Neiderman

This edition first published 2005

Franklin Watts
96 Leonard Street
London EC2A 4XD

Franklin Watts Australia
45-51 Huntley Street
Alexandria NSW 2015

© Franklin Watts 1998

Editor: Samantha Armstrong
Series Designer: Kirstie Billingham
Illustrator: Gemini Patel
Religious Education Consultant: Margaret Barratt, Religious Education Lecturer and author
Buddhist Consultant: Ronald Maddox, General Secretary, The Buddhist Society
Reading Consultant: Prue Goodwin, Reading and Language Information Centre, Reading

A CIP catalogue record for this book is available from
the British Library

Dewey Decimal Classification Number 294.3

ISBN 0 7496 6205 0

Printed in China

Contents

Temples around the world

A Buddhist temple is a place where Buddhists go to learn about the teachings of the **Buddha,** to show respect for him and to be with other Buddhists. There are temples all over the world. Some Buddhist temples are called **viharas.**

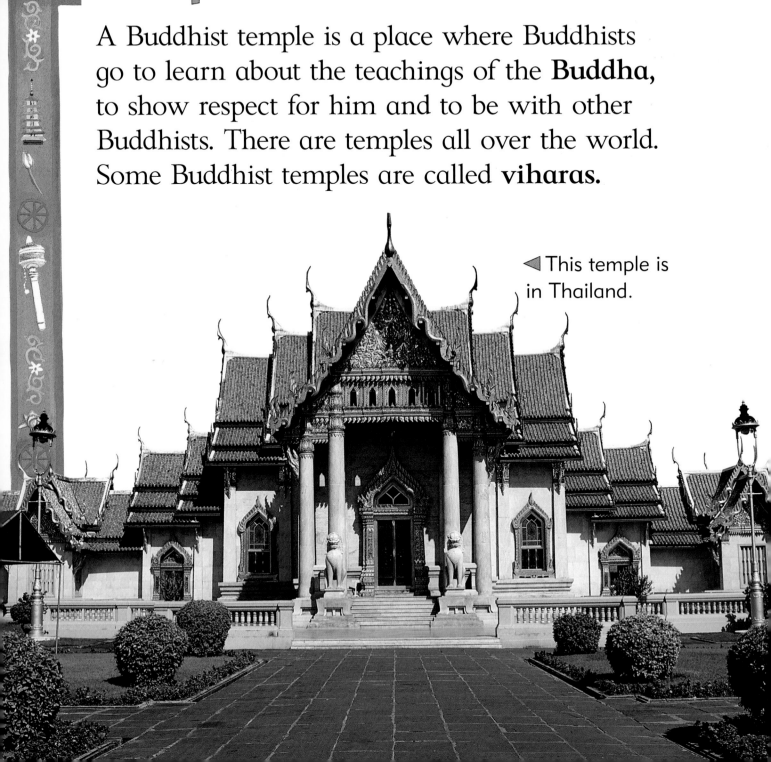

◁ This temple is in Thailand.

Buddhists follow the Buddha's teachings but they do not **worship** him. Pictures or images of the Buddha, called **Buddha rupas**, help Buddhists to remember what the Buddha said and did.

The Buddha is shown in ▷ different positions or **mudras**. Each mudra has a special meaning.

7

The Buddha

The Buddha was born a prince named Siddattha Gotama. He lived in a palace in Nepal. Siddattha had everything he could want, but he felt that there was more to know about life. He went to see what life was like outside the palace. There he saw a sick man, an old man and a dead man. He realised that everyone shared the same problem as the three men. Everyone would suffer and die. He decided to find an answer to this problem.

Many temples have ▷ paintings showing stories from the Buddha's life. This one shows him leaving the palace.

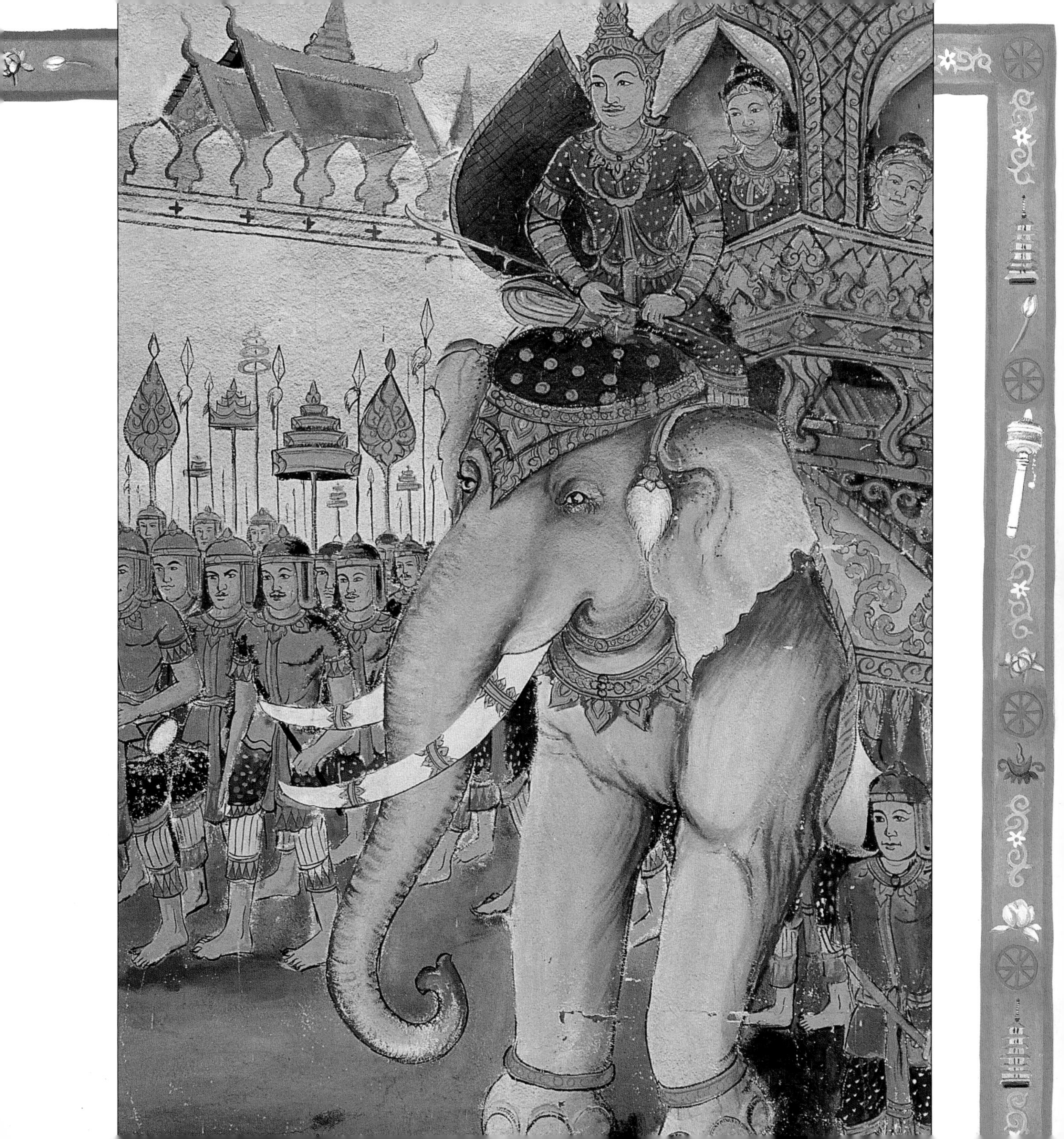

Understanding life

Siddattha met holy men and tried living their strict and simple lives, but he did not find the answer. Then, one day he decided to sit beneath a tree until he understood why people are unhappy and how they can be really wise, peaceful and happy.

When Siddattha realised the answer he was **enlightened.** Buddha means "enlightened one" or "the one who knows".

Here the Buddha is ▷ shown sitting on a bed of lotus flowers. A lotus flower grows out of muddy water. The Buddha said becoming "enlightened" was like growing from muddy water into the light.

10

Inside a temple

Inside a Buddhist temple is a **shrine**. It can be in a special room. The most important part of the shrine is the Buddha rupa. It is in the middle and high up to show how special it is. Buddhists place important things all around the Buddha rupa.

Sometimes there is a model of a pointed mound called a **stupa.** When the Buddha died his ashes and some of his belongings were put inside a huge stupa. Now there are reminders of the Buddha and Buddhist writings in stupas.

Here the Buddha ▷ sits beneath the bodhi tree where he was enlightened. A small stupa is in the corner.

The Three Jewels

Three ideas that are important to Buddhists are called the **Three Jewels.** They are the Buddha, the **Dhamma** and the **Sangha** (the Buddhist community).

◀ These children are making offerings in front of the Buddha rupa. They say the names of the Three Jewels.

The Dhamma

The Dhamma is the name for the Buddha's teachings. The Buddha believed that people cannot be happy if they only think about themselves and their belongings.

The Buddha said these four things about life. They are called the Four Noble Truths:

1. There is unhappiness in life.

2. People are unhappy if they only want their own way.

3. There is a way to end this.

4. The way is called the Noble Eightfold Path. It shows people how to live wisely and happily.

The Noble Eightfold Path

The **Noble Eightfold Path** is shown by a wheel with eight spokes. The Noble Eightfold Path is the Middle Way, not too easy and not too hard. It helps Buddhists to be happy by understanding life, doing good things and making their minds peaceful.

This model of the ▷ Noble Eightfold Path is on top of a temple. The deer on either side of the model remind Buddhists of a speech the Buddha gave in a deer park.

Sangha

Sangha means all the Buddhist **monks** and **nuns** everywhere. It can also mean the whole Buddhist community.
Monks and nuns live a simple life away from their family, just as the Buddha did. They **meditate,** teach the Dhamma and help people. Some do this for their whole lives and others for a short time.

Monks and ▷ nuns have very few possessions. They have a robe, bowl, belt, razor, needle, water filter, a toothpick and a walking stick.

Other Buddhists say thank you to the monks and nuns by giving them food and sometimes robes. This is called **dana.**

Meditation

Meditation is a special kind of thinking. Buddhists meditate to make their minds clear and bright.

When Buddhists practise meditation they kneel or sit cross-legged, sometimes on cushions, and relax. They sit still and quietly, with their eyes closed or slightly open, and they breathe calmly. Some Buddhists say a verse or **mantra** over and over.

Buddhists meditate in ▷ the temple or at home. They meditate on their own or with other people.

◁ Zen Buddhists make special gardens to help them meditate. They have rocks, raked sand or small stones, and maybe a few trees.

21

Puja

One way that Buddhists show their respect for the Buddha is through **puja.** They take off their shoes and sit or kneel in front of the shrine. Then Buddhists bow their heads and put their hands together. This position is called **anjali**. They say a verse about the Three Jewels:

*"I go to the Buddha as my **refuge**.*

I go to the Dhamma as my refuge.

I go to the Sangha as my refuge."

22

They offer flowers to the Buddha.
The flowers will die which shows that everything in life changes. They light candles because the Dhamma lights up the world. They burn incense because it has a sweet smell, like the sweetness of the Dhamma, and spreads into the world.

incense sticks ▷

◁ candle

23

Metta Sutta

The Metta Sutta are verses about loving kindness. At the end of puja the Metta Sutta is often read or chanted. **Metta** means loving kindness, being peaceful and caring for all living things. The Buddha said that everyone should have metta inside them.

◁ These flags in Tibet show metta being sent out to everyone and everything in the world.

▲ Buddhists in Tibet turn wheels with
mantras on them to send goodness into
the world.

A school in a temple

In most Buddhist temples there are classes for children. They learn the Dhamma, often from a monk or nun. They also learn how to meditate and how to lead a Buddhist life.

Here children ▷ are learning about the Three Jewels.

▽ In the past, the Buddha's teachings along with rules for monks and nuns were written on narrow pieces of palm leaves that were threaded together into books.

Glossary

anjali	the postion for showing respect
Buddha	the "enlightened one", he was born Siddattha Gotama
Buddha rupa	an image of the Buddha
dana	giving monks and nuns food, clothes and sometimes shelter
Dhamma	the Buddha's teachings
enlightened	seeing things clearly and wisely
Four Noble Truths	what the Buddha taught about suffering and how to end it
mantra	a word or phrase that is repeated over and over to calm the mind
meditate	to make the mind clear and calm
metta	loving kindness
monks	men who leave their family to teach the Dhamma

mudras   the different positions the Buddha is shown in his Buddha rupa

Noble Eightfold Path   the Buddhist way to find happiness

nuns   women who leave their family to teach the Dhamma

puja   the name of a service and a Buddhist word for showing respect

refuge   safety and support

Sangha   Buddhist monks and nuns. It can also mean the whole Buddhist community

shrine   a Buddha rupa surrounded by offerings

stupa   a mound-shaped building in which things to remind Buddhists about the Buddha are kept

Three Jewels   the Buddha, the Dhamma and the Sangha

vihara   the place where monks and nuns live

Index

Photographic acknowledgements:
Cover: Ann and Bury Peerless; Steve Shott Photography
Insides P6 Ann and Bury Peerless
P7 AKG
P9 Jean-Leo Dugast, Panos Pictures
P11 Jean-Leo Dugast, Panos Pictures
P17 Trip / B. Vikander
P20 Jim Holmes, Panos Pictures
P22 Dominic Sanson, Panos Pictures
P23 Christophe Bluntzer, Impact
All other photographs are by Steve Shott Photography
With thanks to Ven. Somaratana and everyone at the Thames Meditation Centre, Croydon